Guide to Why We Shouldn't Call Our Ancestors Slaves

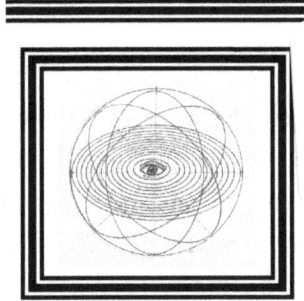

Guide to: Why We Shouldn't Call Our Ancestors Slaves
Copyright © 3/31/2013
by LaRue Nedd, BLD
Published by FNNC Publishing
ISBN: (978-0-9856896-1-2)

(Note: in reference to: Why We Shouldn't Call Our Ancestors Slaves, 3rd Edition, ISBN-10: 0985689609, ISBN-13: 978-0-9856896-0-5, LCCN: 2012953343

How to use this guide

The aim of this guide is to help people familiarize their selves with the information in **Why We Shouldn't Call Our Ancestors Slaves**.

Therefore, I suggest that you go to the back of the book first to see the answers to the questions in the front of the book. Then, go to the front to see if you can answer the questions without seeing the answers. I also suggest that you photo copy the questions so that you can use them as many times as you want.

The answers given in this booklet are not necessarily the only answers that fit the questions. You can see how the answers were developed by going to **Why We Shouldn't Call Our Ancestors Slaves**. The page numbers in the Q & A section refers to the pages in the book.

The following are quotes from the *Mis-Education of the Negro* by Carter G. Woodson. It was written in 1933 and is applicable to this day. In the introduction, he writes:

No systematic effort toward change has been possible, for taught the same economics, history, philosophy, literature and religion, which have established the present code of morals, the Negro's mind has been brought under the control of his oppressor. The problem of holding the Negro down, therefore, is easily solved. When you control a man's thinking you do not have to worry about his actions. You do not have to tell him not to stand here or go yonder. He will find his "proper place" and will stay in it. You do not need to send him to the back door. He will go without being told. In fact, if there is no back door, he will cut one for his special benefit. His education makes it necessary.

The same educational process which inspires and stimulates the oppressor with the thought that he is everything and has accomplished everything worth-while, depresses and crushes at the same time the spark of genius in the Negro by making him feel that his race does not amount to much and never will measure up to the standards of other people. The Negro thus educated is a hopeless liability of the race.

Carter G. Woodson
The Mis-Education of the Negro

From the introduction of *Why We Shouldn't Call Our Ancestors Slaves*, pg 10:

Today, the propaganda machine is even more pervasive and effective in mis-educating us about us and projecting negative images of Black people. Their messages are subtle and subliminal. Almost every Black African American activist recognizes that the images of Black people being projected today are only updated versions of those projected during slavery and the Jim Crow era.

If we accept these negative images as true, we will act accordingly, making what we believe come true. Then, these beliefs become self-fulfilling beliefs. As a result, these negative images cause us to suffer disproportionately in the land of plenty.

Because we have been bombarded with information that says our ancestors were slaves, it is not enough just to say that our ancestors were not slaves. We must understand the logic and the effect that the word slave has on the psyche of Black people. Our children must know that their ancestors were not slaves and that they are not the descendents of a totally defeated people -- slaves. People act according to what they think they are. If we believe that we are the descendents of slaves, how will we act?

No healing can take place until the illness is acknowledged and understood.

Do you remember how you felt the first time you learned that you were the descendant of a people who were slaves to White people?

Have you ever heard or learned that White people use to think that Black people were inferior to White people?

Do you believe that Black people were docile under slavery?

Q-1: Is calling our ancestors slaves a matter of semantics? What is semantics? (Answer on pg. 17)

INTRODUCTION

Q-2: Can money heal the self-esteem issues that plague rich and poor Black people?

    A: _____

Q-3: Why does the belief that our ancestors were slaves affect all Black people? (Answer on pg. 17)

    A: _____

Q-4: What is the logic of the Good Tree? (Answer on pg. 17)

    A: _____

    _____

    _____

PRINCIPLES OF THOUGHT AND ACTION (Answers on pg. 18)

Q-5: Common thoughts and beliefs will produce common_____.

Q-6: Common actions will produce common _____.

THE ISSUES (Answers on pg. 18)

The Intent of Slavery

Q-7: What changes did slavery have on us that are still with us today?

    A: _____

    A: _____

    A: _____

    A: _____

    A: _____

    A: _____

Q-8: What was the primary intent and function of slavery? (Answer on pg. 18)

    A: _____

    A: _____

    A: _____

    A: _____

    A: _____

Q-9: What institutions sanctioned slavery and promoted the belief that Black African people were inferior?

    A: _____, _____,

_____, _____.

Q-10: What was Jim Crow and when was the Jim Crow era? (Answer on pg. 19)

A: _____

_____

A: _____

Q-11: When did the Civil Rights movement begin and end? (Answers on pg. 19)

A: _____

UNDERSTANDING THE DEFINITIONS

Note: Slavery is a system or type of servitude. Not all forms of human servitude are slavery. We would not call soldiers slaves. **Slavery** is the system and the **slave** is the intended product.

The Definition of Slave (Answer on pg. 19)

Q-12: By definition, is it possible to make someone a "slave?"

A: _____

Q-13: What are some of the key phrases in the definition of the noun slave?

A: _____

A: _____

A: _____

A: _____

A: _____

The Connotative Meaning - Slave

Q-14: If it were possible to make someone a slave, how would that person act? (Answers on pg. 20)

A: _____

_____

_____

_____

Word History - Slave (Answers on pg. 20)

From Sclave and Slav to Slave

Q-15: To what does the word sclave refer?

A: _____

_____

Q-16: When was the word slave (spelled s l a v e) first used in the English Language? (Answer on pg. 20)

A: _____

Q-17: Why did they change the spelling from sclave to slave?

A: _____

_____

Q-18: When did the European African Maafa, Trans Atlantic Slave Trade, begin?

A: _____

A Unique Word and Situation – slavery (Answers on pg. 21)

Q-19: What makes "slavery" different from prior forms of servitude?

A: _____

_____

_____

A: _____

The Adjusted Definition – Slave (Answers on pg. 21)

Q-20: Can a person own another person?

A: _____

Q-21: What are the key phrases in the adjusted definitions of the word slave?

A: _____

A: _____

A: _____

A: _____

WHY WE SHOULDN'T CALL OUR ANCESTORS SLAVES

Reason I - The definition does not fit

Q-22: Why is the word slave a bogus word? (Answers on pg 21)

A: _____

A: _____

A: _____

Q-23: Is it possible to make someone a slave?

A: _____Why? _____

_____

Q-24: If it were not a bogus word, why would the definition still not fit? (Answer on pg. 22)

A: _____

_____

A: _____

Q-25: What chain of events was set into motion because of our resistance? (Answers on pg. 22)

A: _____

A: _____

A: _____

A: _____

Reason II - Effect on Mind and Esteem (Answers on pg. 22)

Q-26: We act according to what we think we are, <u>true</u> or <u>false.</u>

A: _____

Q-27: On a scale of 1 – 5, (5 being most important), how important is self-esteem?

A: _____ Why? _____

_____

A: _____

Q-28: Why does calling our ancestors slaves have a negative influence on the psyche and spirit of Black People? (Answer on pg. 23)

A: _____

_____

_____

_____

Q-29: How does calling our ancestors slaves lead to mental disorders among African Americans? (Answer on pg. 23)

A: _____

A: _____

_____

A: _____

Q-30: Calling our ancestors slaves promotes what types of mental disorders? (Answers on pg. 23)

A: _____

A: _____

A: _____

A: _____

Reason III - Abandonment of Form

Q-31: What is meant by form? (Answers on pg. 24)

A: _____

_____

_____

Q-32: What is abandonment of form?

A: _____

_____

Q-33: Why is abandonment of form a twofold problem? (Answer on pg. 24)

A: _____

_____

_____

_____

_____

Q-34: What is culture?

    A: _____

Q-35: What is the cultural transplant?

    A: _____

    _____

Q-36: What is the transplant phenomenon? (Answer on pg. 25)

    A: _____

Q-37: What allegory illustrates the problems with abandonment of form? (Answers on pg. 25)

    A: _____

Q-38: Of all the affects of slavery, the _____ _____ was the most devastating.

Q-39: What sources warn us against abandonment of form?

    A: _____

    A: _____

    A: _____

    A: _____

Reason IV - A Form of Blasphemy

Q-40: What is blasphemy? (Answers on pg. 25)

A: _____

_____

Q-41: Why is calling our ancestors slaves a form of blasphemy?

A: _____

_____

_____

_____

_____

Q-42: What are the <u>main reasons</u> why we should not call our ancestors slaves? (Answers on pg. 26)

A: _____

A: _____

A: _____

A: _____

A: _____

A: _____

IN THE END

Q-43: When we do the right things, we get the _____ _____.

Q-44: Did we sell ourselves into slavery? (Answer on pg 26)

    A: _____

    Reason: _____

    _____

Q-45: As it is applied to our history, according to the dictionary definition, which one is worse a slave or a nigger? (Answer on pg. 26)

    A: _____

Q-46: Were Black people "freed" because White people realized that slavery was wrong? (Answer on pg. 27)

    A: _____

Q-47: What should we call those who act like a slave?

    A: _____

    A: _____

    A: _____

Q-48: What should we call our Ancestors who were caught in slavery? (Answers on pg. 27)

    A: _____

    A: _____

A:_____

A: _____

Questions and Answers

Q-1: Is calling our ancestors slaves a matter of semantics? What is semantics?

A: Yes, it is a matter of semantics. Semantics is the study of the meaning of words, phrases and text.

INTRODUCTION

Q-2: Can money heal the self-esteem issues that plague rich and poor Black people?

A: No

Q-3: Why does the belief that our ancestors were slaves affect all Black people?

A: Because it relates to the people from whom we descended. (pg. 8) And, we will subconsciously apply the logic of the good tree to ourselves.

Q-4: What is the logic of the Good Tree? (pg. 59)

A: Every good tree bears good fruit. Every bad tree bears bad fruit. A good tree cannot bear bad fruit and a bad tree cannot bear good fruit. An apple tree cannot produce oranges. (pg. 59)

PRINCIPLES OF THOUGHT AND ACTION

Q-5: Common thoughts and beliefs will produce common actions.

Q-6: Common actions will produce common results.

THE ISSUES

The Intent of Slavery (pg. 20)

Q-7: What changes did slavery have on us that are still with us today?

A: Religion

A: Language

A: Names

A: Location

A: Family structure

A: World View

Q-8: What was the primary intent and function of slavery? (pg. 20)

A: The intent of slavery was to make Black people the permanent underclass in American society. (pg. 20)

A: The intent of slavery was to cut us off from our mental and spiritual African roots. (pg. 20)

A: To use reward and punishment to control the minds of Black African people so that we would act like slaves.

A: To take out the African mind and replace it with the European mind.

A: To convince Black people that Black people were inferior to Europeans or White people. (pg. 22)

Q-9: What institutions sanctioned slavery and promoted the belief that Black African people were inferior? (pg. 21)

A: the Government,   the church,

the school systems,   the business.

Q-10: What was Jim Crow and when was the Jim Crow era?

A: A set of state and local laws that restricted the movement and conditions of Black people to inferior social conditions.

A: The Jim Crow era was from 1876 to 1965.

Q-11: When did the Civil Rights movement begin and end?

A: 1955 through 1968

UNDERSTANDING THE DEFINITIONS (pg. 29)
Note: Slavery is a system or type of servitude. Not all forms of human servitude are slavery. We would not call soldiers slaves. **Slavery** is the system and the **slave** is the intended product.

The Definition of Slave (pg. 31)

Q-12: By definition, is it possible to make someone a "slave?"

A: No

Q-13: What are some of the key phrases in the definition of the noun slave? (pg. 31)

A: Divested of all freedom

A: Totally and wholly under the control of another

A: Loss of power to resist

A: Owned by another

A: Wholly subject to the will of another

The Connotative Meaning – Slave

Q-14: If it were possible to make someone a slave, how would that person act? (pg. 32)

> A: He or she would have a low level of awareness. He or she would act in the interest of the oppressors and against their own people. He or she would have a self-destructive personality. (pg. 67)

Word History (Slave)

From Sclave and Slav to Slave (pg. 35)

Q-15: To what does the word sclave refer? (pg. 33 – 35)

> A: It refers to the name of a people who lived in Northern Europe known as Slavs. It meant "noble or illustrious."

Q-16: When was the word slave (spelled s l a v e) first used in the English Language?

> A: Around 1538 (pg. 35)

Q-17: Why did they change the spelling from sclave to slave?

> A: to develop a new word to match a form of servitude that had never existed previously.

Q-18: When did the European African Maafa, Trans Atlantic Slave Trade, begin?

> A: in the late 1400's (pg. 36)

A Unique Word and Situation (slavery)

Q-19: What makes "slavery" different from prior forms of servitude? (pg. 37 – 38)

> A: In previous forms of captivity and servitude, captives and bondservants had rights that were covered by the laws of the cultures and society in which they served.

> A: The cultural transplant. (pg. 38)

The Adjusted Definition – Slave

Q-20: Can a person own another person?

> A: No.

Q-21: What are the key phrases in the <u>adjusted definitions</u> of the word slave? (pg. 41)

> A: Chattel

> A: Property

> A: Abjectly subservient

> A: Bondservant. (A bondservant could buy their way out of servitude; a "slave" could not. By definition, a slave would have no desire for "freedom.")

WHY WE SHOULDN'T CALL OUR ANCESTORS SLAVES

Reason I - The definition does not fit (pg. 46)

Q-22: Why is the word slave a bogus word?

> A: Because it is impossible to divest a person of <u>all</u> freedom.

> A: Because it is impossible to take <u>total</u> control of a person.

A: Because, all human beings are endowed <u>with inalienable rights</u>.

Q-23: Is it possible to make someone a slave? (pg. 47)

A: No. Why: Human beings are endowed by their creator with certain inalienable rights and freedoms. Therefore, it is impossible to make someone a slave.

Q-24: If it were not a bogus word, why would the definition still not fit?

A: Because of our overwhelming and relentless resistance to slavery (pg. 48-52) By definition, a slave would not have the will or the power to resist slavery. (pg. 30)

A: At one time, in one way or another all African Black people resisted slavery. All had a desire to be "free." (pg. 47 – 52)

Q-25: What chain of events was set into motion because of our resistance? (pg. 52)

A: Negrophobia -- from the fear of uprisings.

A: Talk of Emancipation prior to the Civil War.

A: The Gag Rule in Congress 1836. (pg 53)

A: Secession of the states from the Union, which lead to the Civil War.

Reason II - Effect on Mind and Esteem

Q-26: We act according to what we think we are, <u>true</u> or <u>false</u>.

A: true.

Q-27: On a scale of 1 – 5, (5 being most important), how important is self-esteem?

    A: 5.   Why? Because self-esteem controls what we can and cannot accomplish.

    A: It is essential for psychological survival. (pg. 66)

Q-28: Why does calling our ancestors slaves have a negative influence on the psyche and spirit of Black People?

    A: It suggests that Black African Americans are the descendents of a powerless people who accepted slavery without a fight. It suggests that Black African Americans are the descendants of an inferior people who can never really win in spite of all of our accomplishments.

Q-29: How does calling our ancestors slaves lead to mental disorders among African Americans?

    A: It leads to identity conflict and disorders. (pg. 67)

    A: Because it prompts African Americans to disconnect from our mental and spiritual sources, our African heritage, our ancestors, and our history. (pg. 71)

    A: It leads to low and negative self-esteem in Black people by association to our ancestors by believing that we are the descendants of an inferior people. (pg. 66)

Q-30: Calling our ancestors slaves promotes what types of mental disorders? (pg. 68)

    A: The Alien Self Disorder

    A: The Anti-self disorder

    A: The Self Distructive Disorders

A: Organic Disorders – Considering that there is a direct relation between mind and body.

Reason III - Abandonment of Form

Q-31: What is meant by form? (pg. 70)

A: Form is the order that dictates the details of a culture or religion. It is the basic pattern that makes a duck a duck, a chicken a chicken and an African an African.

Q-32: What is abandonment of form?

A: It means giving up one's own form with the intent of not returning to it. (pg. 70)

Q-33: Why is abandonment of form a twofold problem?

A: Abandonment of form is a twofold problem: 1) of being separated from the forms to which we had become accustomed and 2) of taking on the forms of a people who are as different from us as black is from white. (pg.71)

Q-34: What is culture?

A: It is the actions that come from the mental and spiritual forms of a society or a people.

Q-35: What was the cultural transplant? (pg. 38)

A: Taking out one culture and replacing it with another. In our case, it is the removal of the African culture and replacing it with the European culture. (note: It is not the same as mixing or the infusion of cultures.)

Q-36: What is the transplant phenomenon? (pg. 79)

A: It is when a body or system rejects a foreign organism or system that has been transplanted.

Q-37: What allegory illustrates the problems with abandonment of form?

A: The chicken and the duck allegory (pg. 72)

Q-38: Of all the affects of slavery, the cultural transplant was the most devastating. (pg.73)

Q-39: What sources warn us against abandonment of form?

A: The Declaration of Independence (pg. 74)

A: "Natural Magic" by Francoise Strachan, pg. 85, (pg 75)

A: KJV of the Bible: Deuteronomy 13:6. (pg. 76)

A: African Religions and Philosophy, 2nd ed, pg. 80. (pg. 87)

Reason IV - A Form of Blasphemy (pg. 82)

Q-40: What is blasphemy?

A: Blasphemy is speaking negatively, insulting or showing contempt toward something that is sacred or reverent.

Q-41: Why is calling our ancestors slaves a form of blasphemy?

A: The word slave implies inferiority and has a dehumanizing meaning. Our ancestors are part of the process that brought us into existence. That which brought us into existence is sacred. Therefore, ignoring or rejecting our history and calling our ancestors slaves is a form of blasphemy. (pg. 88)

Q-42: What are the <u>main reasons</u> why we should not call our ancestors slaves? (pg. 27 & 92)

A: **The definition does not fit**.

A: It is **a bogus word**.

A: It has a **negative effect on the psyche and spirit** of Black people.

A: It is a form of **blasphemy** which is a sin against the spirit of Black people.

A: It leads to **abandonment of form** which causes conflicts in our identity and self-esteem.

A: It **promotes mental disorders** among African Americans.

IN THE END

Q-43: When we do the right things, we get the <u>right</u> <u>results.</u>

Q-44: Did we sell ourselves into slavery? (pg 104)

A: No.

Reason: African people had no concept of the form of human servitude as it was practiced by Europeans, which was called "slavery."

Q-45: As it is applied to our history, according to the dictionary definition, which one is worse a slave or a nigger?

A: Compare definitions in the dictionary. Compare the implied meanings. Come to your own conclusion.

Q-46: Were Black people "freed" because White people realized that slavery was wrong?

A: No. They knew it was wrong when they started it and called it "a necessary evil." They had to abolish "slavery" because of our resistance to it. (pg. 101)

Q-47: What should we call those who act like a slave?

A: We could call them mentally and spiritually ill.

A: We could call them possessed by the European culture.

A: We could say they have an identity disorder or that they are identity challenged.

Q-48: What should we call our ancestors who were caught in slavery? (pg. 107)

A: African prisoners in slavery

A: African prisoners of American slavery

A: American Maafa captives

A: Maafa freedom fighters in America

A: African captives in America

A: Victims of the African Holocaust

Note: As far as this writer is concerned at this time, it really does not matter what terms we use as long as we do not call them slaves or use terms that imply absolute submission or inferiority. Any combination of the above terms will do. But, whatever terms we use, we should be able to identify with our ancestors.

Suggested resources on pg. 111-113

www.ingramcontent.com/pod-product-compliance
Lightning Source LLC
Chambersburg PA
CBHW060606030426
42337CB00019B/3631